The Art of Stoic Negotiation

Navigating Conflict with Patience

Table of Contents

Chapter 1. Introduction

Unveil the secret of serenity in the face of conflict with our Special Report: "The Art of Stoic Negotiation: Navigating Conflict with Patience". This enlightening guide will equip you with the wisdom of ancient Stoic philosophers, adapted to today's negotiation tables. Unravel the strategies to maintain calm, poise, and steadfastness even amidst the stormiest disputes. This isn't just a handbook on newfound patience; it's a transformative journey that will reshape your approach to conflict, infusing it with tranquility and effectiveness. Let's dive into a world where fortitude meets diplomacy, all while keeping a cheerful spirit. Purchase this Special Report, and become the negotiator everyone admires — firm but fair, grounded, yet flexible. Embrace the art of conflict tranquility today!

Chapter 2. Unearthing the Roots of Stoicism

Stoicism, one of the most influential philosophies to hail from the ancient world, offers us a blueprint for enduring hardship and achieving peace of mind. It can be traced back to Athens in 300 BCE, founded by Zeno of Citium, a merchant-turned-philosopher who was influenced by the teachings of Socrates and the Cynics.

2.1. The Life and Influence of Zeno

Zeno's life took a dramatic turn when he was shipwrecked near Athens. He lost nearly everything. But in the grand tradition of Greek philosophy turning perceived misfortune into transformative possibilities, Zeno walked into a bookshop and was introduced to the philosophy of Socrates. He was so inspired that he decided to stay in Athens and devote himself to philosophy.

Zeno began teaching in the Stoa Poikile (Painted Porch), from which the term 'Stoicism' originates. His teachings attracted a considerable following, despite his emphasis on ascetic practices such as indifference to pain and pleasure, and a disciplined control of desires.

2.2. Stoicism's Evolution

Post Zeno, Stoicism was further developed by Cleanthes, Zeno's student, and then Chrysippus, who is known for his considerable contributions to Stoic logic. Stoicism later traversed to the Roman Empire where it thrived, consumed by powerful figures like Seneca, Epictetus, and the Roman Emperor Marcus Aurelius.

2.3. Seneca and His Wisdom

Seneca was born in Corduba but was brought up in Rome, where he achieved fame as a writer, philosopher, and statesman. His works are renowned for their insightful presentation of Stoic doctrine and pragmatic wisdom, particularly concerning the importance of tranquility, the dangers of passions like anger, and the benefits of a simple life.

2.4. Epictetus: The Slave-Turned-Philosopher

Epictetus was born a slave in Hierapolis (present-day Pamukkale in Turkey). After earning his freedom, he moved to Nicopolis in Greece, where he taught philosophy. Epictetus' teachings, as recorded by his student Arrian, form the basis of the Enchiridion, a manual of Stoicism. He expounded the need for personal discipline and emphasized the dichotomy of control, arguing that understanding what is within our control and what's not is key to a good life.

2.5. Marcus Aurelius: The Philosopher Emperor

Last but not least, Marcus Aurelius, the Roman emperor, is considered one of the significant figures promoting Stoicism. His personal writings, assembled in the Meditations, showcase deep-rooted Stoic principles.

2.6. Core Tenets of Stoicism

Stoicism rests on the belief that we don't control and cannot rely on external events. Instead, we can only control ourselves and our responses. By internalizing this principle, Stoics believe, it's possible to attain absolute freedom and tranquility. It differentiates between things 'up to us'—those we control, like behavior and judgments—and things 'not up to us,' like the natural world or others' opinions.

On this note, we hope to have set the stage to understand how Stoic philosophy operates in practical scenarios, specifically negotiation and conflict resolution, where the ability to control one's reactions is a valuable asset.

2.7. Stoicism in Daily Life

Stoicism as a way of life is not about eliminating emotions but restructuring our response to our emotions and experiences. It teaches us that the path to happiness lies in accepting the moment as it presents itself, not allowing oneself to be controlled by the desire for pleasure or the fear of pain.

Through each of these figures—Zeno, Seneca, Epictetus, and Marcus Aurelius—we see a common thread; the overlap of control and peace. As we move forward in this report, this resilient yet tranquil foundation of Stoicism will serve as the bedrock of our explorations into conflict resolution and negotiation in the following chapters.

2.8. To Conclude: Stoicism as Our Guide

So, as we delve deeper into Stoicism and its practice at the negotiation table, remember that it's about more than enduring hardship with a straight face. It's a profound and practical path to maintaining tranquility and effectiveness in the face of demands, disputes, and difficulties of all kinds. In the following sections, we will unveil how these roots of Stoicism provide us the perfect grounding to handle any challenge at the negotiation table.

Chapter 3. An In-depth Look at Stoic Philosophy

The ancient Stoics were not simply philosophers; they were practitioners. To them, philosophy wasn't just an intellectual activity, it was a way of life designed to guide humans in leading a fulfilling existence. Our in-depth exploration of Stoic philosophy begins with its origins, its pillars, and the wisdom it presents for negotiating in life.

3.1. The Origins of Stoic Philosophy

Stoicism was founded by Zeno of Citium in the early 3rd century BCE. Born in Cyprus, Zeno was originally a merchant. After suffering a shipwreck, he arrived in Athens, where he discovered a new philosophical horizon. He began studying with the Cynics, whose emphasis on virtue and simple living greatly influenced him. Eventually, he formed his school of philosophy on the painted porch, or 'stoa,' which is how 'Stoicism' got its name.

3.2. The Pillars of Stoic Philosophy

Stoic philosophy rests on some main pillars, including: the primacy of virtue, the indifference of external things, and the concept of living in accordance with nature.

1. **The Primacy of Virtue**: According to the Stoics, virtue is the highest form of wealth. It is unyielding and cannot be tarnished by external circumstances or personal failures. Thus, a life lived virtuously is the highest good.

2. **The Indifference of External Things**: Stoics firmly believed that our reactions to events are more important than the events themselves. A stoic would apply reason to understand the

occurrence and then respond with wisdom, accepting what cannot be changed.

3. **Living in Accordance with Nature**: To the Stoics, nature is not just the physical world, but the entire cosmos, and its rational structure. To live in harmony with nature is to fully accept our role within the world and to act in accordance with it.

3.3. The Stoic Virtues: Wisdom, Courage, Justice, and Temperance

According to Stoicism, virtue is a singular entity manifesting into different aspects and expressed through four cardinal virtues: wisdom, courage, justice, and temperance.

1. **Wisdom**: The Stoics believed wisdom to be the foundational virtue. It is the ability to distinguish between what is in our control and what isn't, enabling us to navigate life effectively.

2. **Courage**: Stoic courage isn't confined to physical bravery but extends to moral courage, the willingness to stand up for what is right even in the face of adversity.

3. **Justice**: To the Stoics, justice meant treating all human beings with dignity and fairness, regardless of their behavior towards oneself.

4. **Temperance**: Temperance, or moderation, is the virtue of self-restraint, enabling one to desire and act appropriately, avoiding excesses.

3.4. Applying Stoic Philosophy in Negotiation

Stoicism has compelling applications in the realm of negotiation. Predicaments, conflicting interests, and high-stakes decisions - the stormy seas of negotiation can be navigated calmly by adhering to Stoic principles.

1. **Detachment from outcomes**: Treating negotiable items as indifferent allows one to remain focused and not be swayed by emotional impulses. This doesn't mean not caring about the outcome, rather it's about focusing on what one can control, like preparation, execution, and behavior during the negotiation.

2. **Empathy and Understanding**: Being just and fair to the opposing party is crucial. Justice requires understanding their viewpoint and acknowledging their interests. This tends to lower defenses, opening doors for genuine dialogue and collaboration.

3. **Practicing Courageous Patience**: Having the courage to endure drawn-out negotiations and patience to wait for the right opportunity is crucial. Conversely, it's about having the courage not to rush into suboptimal agreements in the interest of time.

4. **Applying wisdom through Emotional Intelligence**: Stoic wisdom comes to play in recognizing one's own emotions and those of others, choosing the appropriate response. Also, the wisdom to understand what is and isn't negotiable, to prioritize issues properly, and to be flexible where possible.

Stoic philosophy is a rich treasure of ancient wisdom that can revolutionize how we think, feel, and behave in the face of conflict and strife. Its application in negotiation is manifold. By practicing Stoic tenets, one can calmly navigate the volatile seas of negotiation, weathering storms with poise and reaching outcomes that uphold human dignity and fairness. Harnessing the power of Stoicism can transform not just our negotiating skills but our approach to life.

Chapter 4. Stoic Ethics - The Pathway to Patience

Stoicism, an ancient philosophical tradition, has served as an important beacon to humanity, illuminating the path towards patience, virtue, and tranquility. Its teachings have stood the test of time and are as relevant today as they were during the reign of emperors.

4.1. A Difficult Virtue: Understanding Patience

Patience is a virtue that most of us struggle with. Whether it's waiting in line at the supermarket or waiting for a significant life event, impatience seems innately woven into our character. Yet, the Stoics viewed patience as a cornerstone of a tranquil life. The Greek philosopher Epictetus once claimed, "Bear in mind that it is not the man who reviles or strikes you who insults you, but it is your judgment about these things as being insulting."

In this light, it's clear that patience isn't simply the act of waiting, but it's the manner in which one waits. It's about maintaining serenity, poise, and a rational perspective even when faced with events that don't proceed as per our wishes. This virtue becomes particularly vital during negotiations, as patience can be the key that decides whether you lose your cool or maintain a level-headed perspective.

4.2. Stoic Ethics: Virtue is the Highest Good

At the heart of Stoic philosophy is the belief that virtue is the highest good. Virtue encompasses the qualities of wisdom, bravery, justice, and temperance. Each of them is interdependent and contributes to the formation of a virtuous, balanced individual. Among these, temperance, or the ability to control one's desires and impulses, plays a pivotal role in cultivating patience.

Stoics believe that we can't control everything in our lives. However, we can control our reactions to events. When we comprehend this fully, we begin to respond to situations rather than react, allowing wisdom and patience to guide us in all circumstances. By accepting and working with reality, instead of fighting or resisting it, we naturally cultivate patience.

4.3. The Dichotomy of Control

The Stoic philosophy contains an important tenet known as the 'Dichotomy of Control'. This principle revolves around the idea that some things are within our control (our thoughts, beliefs, actions) while others are not (other people's actions, natural events). Comprehending this dichotomy is a crucial step towards embodying patience.

By accepting this fundamental, we save ourselves from unnecessary frustration caused by trying to control the uncontrollable. This acceptance not only brings equanimity but also enriches our patience.

Take a negotiation, for example. You might have done all the necessary preparation, but the other party is being unreasonably stubborn. Instead of letting frustration erode your patience, Stoicism would advise you to recognize what's within your sphere of control. You can't change their behavior, but you can control your reaction to it. This understanding preserves your calm and cultivates patience in the face of adversity.

4.4. Seeing through the Stoic Lens: Objective Representation

In the quest to nurture patience, Stoicism proposes a strategy called 'Objective Representation.' This is the practice of seeing things as they truly are, minus any personal bias or subjective interpretation. It's about breaking events down to their bare essentials, which enables a certain distance that helps you remain patient and resilient against the whirlwind of emotions that might otherwise engulf you during conflict.

Imagine you are in a negotiation where the discussions are turning heated. Instead of reacting immediately, you deconstruct the situation: What exactly is the person saying? What is the impact of it on the negotiation? This objective analysis can help to deescalate the situation, preserving the virtue of patience and keeping the negotiation on track.

4.5. Emotional Resilience: Our True Shield

Stoics saw emotions not as barriers but as navigable pathways leading towards virtue. Seeing patience as an emotional resilience tool, they believed that we could wield this shield to fortify ourselves against disruptive external forces.

Marcus Aurelius, an iconic stoic philosopher and emperor, famously wrote: "Today I escaped from anxiety. Or no, I discarded it, because it was within me, in my own perceptions—not outside." The lesson here is profound. Patience isn't something we acquire in the external world; it's something we cultivate within ourselves. It can empower negotiators to manage their emotions more effectively, allowing space for logic and reason to guide their decision-making.

Learning to embody the wisdom of Stoic ethics is like learning an art. It takes practice, perseverance, and patience. Yet, the rewards are manifold, enabling us to navigate conflict with an unruffled mind, giving us the ability to stay composed, and opening new horizons for successful negotiation. The path of patience may seem demanding at first, but the journey can become a transformative one, offering insights about our inner selves and the world around us, making us more resilient negotiators and more tranquil human beings.

Remember, according to Stoic ethics, the pursuit of patience isn't about eliminating all feelings of annoyance or frustration. Rather, it revolves around channeling these feelings into a constructive form, enabling us to act in a virtuous way essentially exhibiting wisdom, justice, bravery, and temperance. By doing this, we can reach a state of unshakable patience, allowing us to approach every negotiation with clarity and calm. In a world preoccupied with immediate results and quick fixes, the Stoic lesson of patience stands out as timeless wisdom, allowing us to calmly navigate the rough waters of every conflict with serenity and determination.

Chapter 5. Translating Stoicism into the Act of Negotiation

To grasp the significance of integrating Stoic philosophy into negotiation practices, we first need to delve into the core tenets of Stoicism and their pertinence to the act of negotiation.

Stoicism, founded by Zeno of Citium in the early 3rd century BC, esteems logic, personal ethics, and virtue as chief virtues obtained by submission to reasoning. Simply put, Stoicism teaches us to differentiate between things we can control - our responses, judgments, values, and conduct - and things we can't control, such as the actions, thoughts, and attitudes of others.

For a negotiator, these teachings can be instrumental in maneuvering through the twists and turns that negotiations often entail, remaining equanimical, and making decisions based on logic and rational assessment.

5.1. Stoic Philosophy And Its Relevance To Negotiation

Dovetailing the Stoic philosophy with the act of negotiation presents us with a potent tool that can steer our approach and conduct during negotiations. Let's dissect the four cardinal virtues of Stoicism - wisdom, justice, courage, and temperance - and their bearing on negotiation:

- Wisdom: It is the understanding of what is good, evil, and what lies indifferent between them. In negotiation, the wisdom to discern obstructions and opportunities can guide you to make more effective decisions.

- Justice: It is the knowledge of the distribution of proper due. A negotiator, rooted in the virtue of justice, would be intent on a fair agreement that respects and advocates the parties' rights and obligations.

- Courage: This refers to facing everyday life challenges without fear, yet with wisdom. A stoic negotiator would exhibit the courage to put forth firm arguments, defend their points, and gracefully accept rejections.

- Temperance: It is the voluntary self-restraint from harmful overindulgences. A temperate negotiator, being in command of his cravings and emotions, can circumvent potential heated confrontations, thus preserving a harmonious negotiation ambiance.

It's worth noting that Stoicism is not about curbing emotions utterly; instead, it's about regulating our responses to external influences for inner peace.

5.2. Stoic-related Techniques For Effective Negotiation

Now that we've discussed Stoic philosophy's foundational principles, we'll explore how you can incorporate these principles into your negotiation strategies.

Dispassionate Approach: Embrace objectivity and view the situation without unnecessary emotional involvement. By detaching yourself from the potential outcomes of the negotiation - success or failure - you free yourself from the dread of a non-favourable result. You devote your mental energy to creating persuasive arguments and counter-arguments instead.

Reframe Perception: In the face of conflicts, attempt to reframe your perception. This can be achieved by embracing a Stoic technique called Premeditatio Malorum — the premeditation of evils. It involves contemplating the occasions when negotiations could lead to adverse outcomes, thereby preparing your mind to stay calm and resilient, should these situations transpire.

Utilize The Dichotomy of Control: By focusing on variables you can control in a negotiation (your preparation, presentation, and demeanor) and accepting the elements you cannot (the other party's disposition, actions, or decisions), you preserve your peace of mind and steer your energy towards productive aspects.

5.3. Forming a Stoic Mindset: Practical Exercises

Developing a Stoic mindset isn't an overnight venture. It requires consistent practice and commitment. However, a few exercises practiced regularly can assist in this journey.

Reflective Journaling: Document your thoughts, fears, impressions, and expectations concerning the negotiation. Reflect upon them and rationally assess their authenticity. This self-awareness can aid you in managing your emotional responses judiciously.

Virtue Signalling: Reinforce the four Stoic virtues — wisdom, justice, courage, and temperance — repeatedly. Recall instances from past negotiations where you've exhibited these virtues and draw inspiration from the same.

Meditate: Engage in mindfulness or meditative practices. They allow you to maintain your calm, compose your thoughts, and approach negotiations from a place of balance and objectivity.

5.4. The Stoic Negotiator: Bringing It All Together

A Stoic negotiator is pensive and deliberate. Upholding the principles of justice, they aim for an equitable outcome that respects both parties' interests. They exhibit a dispassionate approach, ensuring to not let personal biases and emotions sway their judgment. Confident and vulnerable at the same time, they possess the courage to portray their points assertively and the humility to accept counter-arguments gracefully. And most importantly, they embrace the dichotomy of control, focusing on the aspects within their command, and accepting the things beyond.

Translating Stoicism into the act of negotiation can be a transformative realignment of thought and approach. With perseverance, consistent practice, and dedication to employing Stoic principles at the negotiation tables, the journey forward is not just for improved negotiation skills but indeed for better, more serene life experiences. By internalizing the essence of Stoicism, you have a chance to bring serenity into the heart of conflicts, become a more competent negotiator, and, moreover, a more composed, happier human.

Chapter 6. Cultivating Stoic Patient Practice

In the realm of Stoicism, the pursuit of virtue serves as your compass, guiding you through life's turbulent seas. Virtue, quite often, presents itself as patience—an invaluable trait when negotiating challenging scenarios. To cultivate stoic patience requires a transformation of perspective, practices, and principles, and we begin this journey by gaining understanding of the origin of impatience.

6.1. The Philosophy of Impatience

Impatience typically emerges from our desire for control—the urge to have everything go exactly as planned. However, such desire misaligns with the natural workings of the world, where determinism rules. The Stoics understood this through the concept of 'Fate', advocating acceptance of reality as it presents itself. To endure patiently involves shifting your viewpoint and accepting both the consequences of your actions and the circumstances outside your influence.

6.2. Recognizing What is Within Your Control

The foundation of Stoic philosophy is understanding what is within your control and what isn't. Epictetus, the renowned Stoic philosopher, proposed that our opinions, desires, rejections, and preparations are firmly within our control, while everything else isn't. The realization of this pivotal principle forms the first step on this journey of cultivating Stoic patience.

6.3. Cultivating the Practice of Premeditatio Malorum

Premeditatio Malorum, a Stoic exercise translating as 'the premeditation of evils', helps them cultivate resilience and patience by visualizing worst-case scenarios. Knowing the potential outcomes—particularly the negative possibilities—can help you prepare and arm you with patience when negotiating.

6.4. Redefining Your View of Time

The essence of patience lies in your perception of time, thus Stoicism calls for an adjustment in this viewpoint. An excerpt from Seneca's 'On The Shortness of Life' provides a compelling paradigm shift, painting time not as fleeting but rather as abundant, only seeming short because of how we use it.

6.5. Stoic Exercises for Patience

Several mechanisms and exercises can sharpen your patience. Developing a mindfulness practice, embracing delay, implementing regular reflection, and modifying your environment can collectively foster patience, one moment at a time.

6.6. Mindfulness Practice

At its core, mindfulness is about living in the present and appreciating the state of flow. By allowing yourself to immerse fully in each task or conversation, you nurture attentiveness which prepares the ground for patience to blossom. Simple exercises could involve taking deep breaths, yoga, or walking in nature.

6.7. Embracing Delay

Adopting a perspective that cherishes delay, rather than resents it, maximizes your endurance. Using any waiting time as a window for reflection, planning, or simply enjoying the pause can serve as a beneficial patience-conditioning task.

6.8. Regular Reflection

Keeping a Stoic journal where you document your progress and insights proves instrumental in cultivating patience. Periodic reflection can clarify your thoughts, identify growth areas, and ultimately foster a patient mindset in negotiations.

6.9. Modifying Your Environment

Your surroundings shape your attitude more than you might guess. Surround yourself with people, objects, and even literature that embody patience, and use these settings as talismans for slow, thoughtful deliberations.

6.10. Conclusion

To cultivate Stoic patience doesn't entail becoming passive. It's about realizing the futility of resistance against natural flow, understanding the distinction between what you can and cannot control, and employing a set of practices designed to craft patience into your psyche. As you embrace these philosophies and practices, your approach to negotiation and conflict management evolves, transforming you into a person of unwavering patience, infallibly serene amidst the stormiest disputes.

Chapter 7. Case Studies: Stoic Negotiation in Action

In this chapter, we'll examine various instances where Stoic principles have been effectively put into practice during intense negotiations. These instances are not only enlightening but also a source of inspiration and practical applicability for readers.

7.1. The Cuban Missile Crisis: Kennedy's Stoic Bravery

October 1962 marked one of the most nerve-racking periods in human history. The Cuban Missile Crisis found two superpowers, the United States and the Soviet Union, on the brink of nuclear war. The young President John F. Kennedy, with his cabinet of advisors nicknamed ExComm, was attempting to navigate this precarious situation.

Kennedy demonstrated the Stoic value of courage. Not just physical bravery, but also moral courage — a commitment to doing what's right despite the potential for enormous personal or political cost. His ability to maintain a calm demeanor, suppressing his initial shock and panic, reflected the practices that the stoics preach.

When handling the crisis, Kennedy chose a measured response, rather than a full-force military attack. He incorporated reasoned judgment, another Stoic principle, to analyze the situation objectively without letting emotions cloud his decisions. A naval blockade around Cuba was implemented, much less provocative than direct military intervention.

John F. Kennedy's approach to one of history's most tense standoffs exemplifies the practice of Stoic negotiation in action. His cool head, moral courage, and sense of justice are characteristic of a Stoic negotiator.

7.2. The Negotiation of The Good Friday Agreement: Hume's Stoic Temperance

The negotiation process leading to the Good Friday Agreement in Northern Ireland is another excellent example of Stoic negotiation in action. In particular, the role played by John Hume, a key figure in the peace process, stands out for his stoic approach.

A believer in non-violence and political dialogue, Hume demonstrated Stoic qualities of temperance and self-discipline. And despite the regular bouts of violence and animosity, Hume never lost sight of his purpose: the peaceful unification of Ireland.

Over many years, Hume maintained dialogues with all parties involved, engaging not only with political allies and neutral parties but also with those who were firmly in opposition. His ability to separate the negotiators from their contentious positions reflects the Stoic principle of viewing all people as fundamentally rational beings.

Hume's ability to maintain calm and stability during tumultuous times reflects the Stoic virtue of tranquility. His determination throughout the peace process exemplifies the Stoic principle of perseverance, demonstrating how Stoic negotiation can lead to lasting resolutions.

7.3. The Release of Nelson Mandela: De Klerk's Stoic Wisdom

The negotiations for the release of Nelson Mandela and the eventual end of apartheid in South Africa also offer illuminating examples of Stoic negotiation principles in practice. F.W. de Klerk, the last State President of apartheid-era South Africa, was instrumental in this transformative negotiation.

One of the primary principles of Stoicism is wisdom, which includes excellent deliberation, understanding, and resourcefulness. De Klerk exercised such wisdom by recognizing the need for change and initiating negotiations for the end of apartheid.

Despite intense pressure and threats to his personal safety, de Klerk continued dialogue with Mandela and his supporters, maintaining a steadfast stride akin to a stoic walking a virtuous path. Moreover, his understanding that the equal treatment of all South Africans was a matter of justice demonstrates the Stoic virtue of justice.

De Klerk's actions demonstrate the use of Stoic wisdom and justice in negotiations, providing an inspirational lesson in large-scale negotiation and peaceful resolution of incredibly charged conflicts.

In conclusion, these case studies obviously demonstrate how the application of Stoic principles such as wisdom, courage, temperance, and justice can turn around heated dialogues into peaceful resolutions. They showcase the power of maintaining a serene and calm demeanor, separating the negotiators from their positions, maintaining an objective view, and persevering through the negotiation process. This mindset of a Stoic negotiator not only facilitates successful resolution of conflicts but also lays down the foundation for inner peace and self growth.

Chapter 8. Overcoming Conflict: The Stoic Approach

The beginning of the Stoic's journey towards mastering the art of negotiation lies in understanding the nature of conflict itself. Marcus Aurelius, a Stoic philosopher and once Emperor of Rome, said, "You have power over your mind - not outside events. Realize this, and you will find strength." This seems simple, but every negotiation bristles with external events that can influence our internal serenity. Let's explore how Stoicism teaches us to navigate these.

8.1. Unpacking Conflict

Conflict is a part of life. It comes from the Greek word 'konfliktos' which translates to 'striking together'. It is inevitable when two or more perspectives differ and can arise from differences in interests, values, and needs. The Stoics view this as an integral part of human society, as natural occurrences—neither good nor bad. The crux of the matter is how we respond to it. Conflict is potentially an opportunity for growth, creativity, and improved relationships.

8.2. The Power of Perception

Epictetus, a famous Stoic philosopher, asserts, "We are not disturbed by what happens to us, but by our thoughts about what happens to us." This highlights the remarkable control we possess, not over events, but over how we perceive and interpret them. While disagreements are routinely viewed as distressing events, Stoic negotiators view them as challenges that help them grow. The power to interpret conflict lies within you: frame it not as an ordeal, but as an opportunity to demonstrate virtues like patience, resilience, and fairness.

8.3. Embracing Reason over Emotion

When emotions run high, objectivity suffers, and rational conversations falter. Stoicism advises us to respond with reason instead of emotion. Remember your ultimate goal in negotiation: reaching a satisfactory agreement, not assuaging your bruised ego or proving yourself right at all costs. Such a perspective can remarkably diffuse animosity and pave the way for rational dialogue.

8.4. Resisting Retaliation

In the face of heated discussions, resist the urge to be defensive or retaliate. Instead, invite your counterpart to explore your viewpoint, and equally strive to understand theirs. By refusing to engage in a verbal match, you uphold the Stoic values of dignity and respect. Stoic philosophy emphasizes that how others treat us should not determine how we treat them.

8.5. Detachment: Your Shield Against Agitation

Stoics advise us to practice detachment, intertwined with objectivity, to insulate our inner peace in negotiations. Detachment isn't indifference; instead, it's being intensely involved in the negotiation without letting external events impact your inner tranquillity. If the negotiation doesn't proceed as desired, your happiness remains unscathed because your contentment hinges on values and virtues, not the outcome.

8.6. Stoicism in Action: Using the Trichotomy of Control

One of the most substantial contributions of Stoicism to effective negotiation is the Trichotomy of Control. This principle asserts that everything falls into three categories—what we control, what we partly control, and what we cannot control.

The first category encompasses our actions, decisions, and internal emotional states. We can entirely control these. The second category includes events we have partial control over, like negotiations. We can influence the outcome, but it heavily depends on others' decisions. The third category comprises events entirely outside our domain, such as the weather or another person's opinion.

Recognizing these distinctions shields us from unnecessary stress and helps us cultivate serenity in the negotiation process. It permits us to focus on our input rather than obsessing over the outcome.

8.7. Your Toolkit for Tranquility: The Stoic Virtues

The cardinal virtues of Stoicism – wisdom, courage, justice, and temperance – can be potent tools in your negotiation toolkit.

Wisdom allows you to discern the nuances of negotiation, understanding the stakes, empathizing with the other's perspective, and finding common grounds.

Courage is not about physical bravery but about moral courage, standing by your convictions even under pressure.

Justice insists that your negotiation goals not be solely for your benefit but fair and equitable.

Temperance echoes the virtue of restraint, ensuring you refrain from hasty decisions or from being lured by short-term gains, focusing instead on the long-term effects of the negotiation.

Stoicism doesn't promise a conflict-free journey, but it equips us to remain serene in the face of conflict, guiding us toward effective negotiation. Tracing the footprints of ancient Stoics, we can infuse age-old wisdom into modern negotiation strategies to create harmonious relationships grounded in mutual respect and understanding. Thus, we become not just proficient negotiators but also emotionally resilient individuals, modeling the much-needed balance of strength and serenity in our turbulent times.

By understanding, internalizing and practicing these Stoic teachings, we can arm ourselves with a shield – our inner peace – that external conflicts cannot penetrate. This is, indeed, the art of Stoic negotiation: navigating conflict with patience and maintaining our tranquillity no matter the negotiation outcome.

Remember, as Marcus Aurelius declared: "You have power over your mind – not outside events. Realize this, and you will find strength."

May this strength be with you in all your negotiating endeavors, empowering you to transform conflict into constructive collaboration.

Chapter 9. The Stoic Mindset: Building Resilience in Negotiations

The Stoic Mindset is inherently resilient, aimed at developing a strong, adaptive mentality that can withstand any vicissitudes, especially those encountered amidst negotiation tables. Imbued with the wisdom of ancient philosophers such as Seneca, Epictetus, and Marcus Aurelius, the Stoic negotiator's character isn't shaken by external circumstances but remains composed, firm, flexible and just - a powerful beacon in a storm of disputes and disagreements.

9.1. Stoicism: The Resilient Philosophy

Coming from Greek roots, Stoicism emphasizes virtue, wisdom, courage, justice, and temperance. These cornerstones of the philosophy aid us in shaping a robust mindset by focusing on the things we can control and accepting those beyond our realm of influence. It teaches us to be indifferent to emotions that cloud judgement, fostering a clearer thought process necessary for effective negotiation.

Let's consider an essential tenet of Stoicism, the dichotomy of control. It suggests that some things are up to us, and others are not. In negotiations, the things we control are our thoughts, actions, feelings, and reactions. Things we don't control include other people's thoughts, actions, and the ultimate negotiation outcome. Hence, it's crucial to focus on our actions and responses rather than worrying about factors beyond our influence. Embracing this dichotomy not only develops our resilience but also reduces stress and anxiety during negotiations.

9.2. The Indomitable Stoic Virtues

When we think of the resilience cultivated by Stoics, we invariably arrive at the four cardinal virtues: Prudence, Courage, Justice, and Temperance. These are the essential attributes which, when applied to negotiations, result in a balanced, effective, and resilient negotiator.

- Prudence (Wisdom): It is crucial to understand what is good, what is evil, and what is neutral. In a negotiation, wisdom means to discern the right course, identify common interests, and develop effective strategies. It enables us to understand things from others' perspectives, promoting empathy and enhancing communication.

- Courage: It represents confronting fear and pain, not in the physical sense, but on a mental and emotional level. Courage in negotiations means having difficult conversations, asserting oneself, and making and standing by challenging decisions.

- Justice: Being just in Stoicism means acting with integrity, honesty, and treating people fairly. In negotiations, this virtue ensures that our actions are ethical and equitable — fostering trust and a respectful environment.

- Temperance: It signifies moderation and self-control. A tempered negotiator can manage their impulses and emotions, maintain balance, stay calm under pressure, and react appropriately.

The embodiment of these cardinal virtues will aid in the formation of a resilient stoic mindset, capable of navigating the turbulence of negotiations with serenity and efficiency.

9.3. Shaping the Stoic Mindset: Practical Steps

Adopting a stoic mindset isn't an overnight transformation. It requires intentional practice and diligent self-reflection. Here are some practical steps that can help you on this journey:

1. Reflect Daily: Spend time each day contemplating and analyzing your thoughts and actions. Revisit your negotiations and evaluate whether you maintained tranquility and made decisions aligned with Stoic virtues.

2. Practice Discomfort: Train yourself to be comfortable in discomforting scenarios. Regularly engaging with challenging situations enhances resilience and minimizes reactionary behaviors.

3. Apply Negative Visualization: Imagine worst-case scenarios and how you would maintain poise and effectiveness within them. This strategy fosters resilience, reduces anxiety, and prepares you for every possible outcome.

4. Meditate on Stoic Teachings: Regularly revisit Stoic teachings and quotes. Incorporate them into your thought process, allowing them to shape your perspectives and actions.

9.4. The Stoic Mindset in Conflict: An Effective Armor

Negotiations can sometimes assume the shape of intense disputes and conflicts. Here, the Stoic mindset becomes an effective armor, immunizing the negotiator against emotional turmoil and encouraging balanced decisions.

The Stoic negotiator doesn't get carried away by insults, rejections, or challenging demands. Such a negotiator remains anchored to their virtues, staying calm amidst the strain, unflustered by aggressive strategies, and undeterred by unfavorable odds.

Stoicism equips the negotiator with the courage to face conflicts head-on, the wisdom to devise effective strategies, a sense of justice that instills trust, and the temperance that helps stay stable, firm, yet adaptable.

In conclusion, the Stoic mindset isn't merely about resilience; it's about being an effective negotiator who can smoothly navigate conflict waters, who remains unperturbed amidst storms, and who radiates a tranquility that can pacify even the fiercest disputes. Embarking on this Stoic journey calls for the courage to self-reflect, the humility to learn, and the fortitude to remain steadfast amidst adversities - for that is where the art of Stoic negotiation thrives.

Chapter 10. Advanced Techniques in Stoic Negotiation

In the realm of Stoic negotiation, advanced techniques form the linchpin of successful discourse. At the heart of every meaningful discussion and negotiation resolution is the understanding of the need for equanimity, and the ability to remain unperturbed, no matter what. Let's delve deeper into how these core Stoic principles can prove to be game-changers in negotiation scenarios.

10.1. The Four Cardinal Virtues of Stoicism

The Four Cardinal Virtues of Stoicism - wisdom, courage, justice, and temperance often serve as the fundamental guiding pillars of stoic negotiation. Each virtue brings its own valuable contribution to the negotiation table.

Wisdom involves making the best use of available information and recognizing the areas where you lack knowledge. In a negotiation, this can manifest as understanding your counterpart's position, recognizing your own blind spots, and finding a mutually beneficial solution.

Courage is required to steadfastly maintain your just position, even when confronted with threatening or intimidating behaviour. It is the strength that allows you to communicate authentically and assertively without resorting to aggression.

Justice involves treating all parties involved with fairness and respect, which is crucial to maintaining a positive negotiation environment. Remember, 'Adversarial' does not have to mean 'Enemy'.

Temperance is the practice of self-restraint, allowing you to keep hold of your passions and not make rash decisions under pressure.

Moving beyond these fundamental virtues, let us explore more advanced concepts and techniques that can guide your path to becoming a seasoned stoic negotiator.

10.2. Leveraging Dichotomy of Control

The Dichotomy of Control is a central concept in Stoicism that splits everything into two categories: things we can control, and things we can't. In negotiations, being mindful of this dichotomy removes anxiety and unnecessary frustration, thus keeping you focused and calm.

Recognize what is within your control—your actions, reactions, attitudes, and strategies. Accept that there are things beyond your control—how others react, their attitudes, whether the deal closes, etc.

When you focus on the aspects within your control, you can act effectively and with clarity. Conversely, accepting immutable circumstances helps in letting go of unrealistic expectations and curbs unnecessary stress during negotiations.

10.3. Channelling Negative Visualization

Negative visualization involves imagining worst-case scenarios, thereby helping prepare for any possible negotiation outcome.

Visualizing losing a deal or facing difficult situations reduces anxiety, as you're mentally prepared for the worst.

However, this shouldn't be mistaken for pessimism. By mentally rehearsing tough scenarios, you develop the emotional strength to deal with them if they occur. This not only eliminates surprise factors, but also equips you with the confidence to maneuver through complex negotiations.

10.4. Embrace Voluntary Discomfort

Stoics embraced voluntary discomfort to build resilience. This particular practice can help you strengthen your resolve, helping you navigate challenging negotiations. By pushing your boundaries and allowing yourself to experience discomfort, you can increase your tolerance for stress—proactively prepare for longer sessions, challenging questions, or harder bargains. You'll take a seemingly unfavourable situation, and turn it into an opportunity for growth.

10.5. The Role of Practical Wisdom

Often mistaken for theoretical wisdom, practical wisdom in Stoicism is the ability to navigate complex situations ethically and effectively. To make ethical decisions in a negotiation, practical wisdom is indispensable. It guides you toward establishing fairness and ensures you do not compromise your values to win a deal. It helps you balance the act of pursuing your interests and, at the same time, maintaining justice.

By mastering these advanced techniques, you will be better prepared to respond to adversities, effectively reducing the volatility and chaos typically associated with intense negotiations. Using these skills, you'd foster a negotiation environment that is fair, respectful, productive, and above all, calm.

Stoic negotiation is not just about reaching an agreement; it's about reaching it in a way that fosters positivity, mutual respect, and tranquility, while standing firmly on one's virtues and values. Being a Stoic negotiator unravels a path to effective negotiation outcomes, not through the route of aggression, but through the path of wisdom, patience, and serenity.

Chapter 11. The Future of Negotiation: Stoicism in a Modern World

In the rapidly evolving milieu of the 21st century, where everything from trade to technology, from diplomacy to data, exists in a constant state of negotiation, the need for efficacious tools to navigate these shifting planes is more prominent than ever. As we scour through history, philosophy, and wisdom, the teachings of Stoicism, rooted in the tranquillity of the mind and the resilience of spirit, emerge as enormously relevant in bolstering our negotiation prowess. The amalgamation of this ancient philosophy with modern practices can usher in a new era of conflict resolution — where the storm is weathered not with aggression, but with the armor of serenity and wisdom.

11.1. Stoicism: A Retrospective Analysis

Dating back to the 3rd century BCE, Stoicism was born in the bustling marketplace of Athens, brought to the world by its founder Zeno of Citium. Unlike the cloistered philosophical environments such as Plato's Academy or Aristotle's Lyceum, Stoicism truly was the philosophy of the agora — the open marketplace. It taught people to embrace a life of virtue, tolerance, and tranquillity while shunning vices and unnecessary desires.

The Stoics like Epictetus stressed the dichotomy of control, guiding individuals to concentrate on things within one's control and to display indifference towards those that were beyond. This nurtures resilience, enabling us to stay steadfast amid adversities and approach negotiations with serenity, empowering us to make rational decisions.

11.2. Stoicism in Modern Negotiations

Translating ancient Stoic wisdom to modern negotiation tables, we find remarkable synergy. Most negotiations are assailed by volatility, ambiguity, and conflicting interests. In this fray, an individual equipped with Stoic principles can maintain equanimity, perceive things objectively, and thereby steer conversations towards resolutions with minimum friction.

Consider Marcus Aurelius, the Roman Emperor identified often with the Stoic phrase 'Memento Mori' (remember you will die). This reminder of mortality was not meant as a bleak observance of fleeting life but a call to value our time and what we do with it. When translated into the context of negotiations, this calls for focussing on the essentials, avoiding getting caught up in trivialities and maintaining an overarching perspective on achieving resolution rather than victory.

11.3. Stoic Tools for Negotiation

The beauty of Stoicism lies in its provision of practical tools to navigate life, which can also be applied to negotiations. Adopting these tools can equip us with a calm demeanor, clear thought-process, and the ability to objectively analyze situations, leading to productive and fair outcomes.

- Physical Tranquillity: The Stoics regarded tranquillity not a mere state of mind but as something that must also extend to our physical disposition. In negotiations, these means nurturing a calm, composed demeanor that permeates our body language, tone and expressions – subtly influencing the negotiation environment towards a more composed, less confrontational space.

- Virtue and Justice: Stoics believed in the central role of virtue in living a good life. Justice, one of the core Stoic virtues, holds significant importance in negotiations. It requires one to be fair and balanced when dealing with others. It also mandates the acknowledgment of each party's needs and interests, aiding in fostering mutual respect and generating win-win solutions.

- Indifferent to Externals: Stoics prescribed that we should remain indifferent to things outside our control. In negotiating terms, it signifies focusing on our preparation, approach, and behavior rather than obsessing over the outcomes. This fosters not only a stress-free negotiating environment but also aids in clearer decision-making.

11.4. Sailing Against the Wind: Case Studies in Stoic Negotiation

Examining real-life scenarios where leaders have displayed Stoic philosophy in negotiations can provide us with valuable insights. Let's look at the Cuban Missile Crisis, where President John F. Kennedy displayed Stoic principles, particularly, his perception and reaction to events, focusing on that which he could control, responding rather than reacting, and acting virtuously and wisely in the face of grave danger.

Another poignant example is of South African President Nelson Mandela, who showcased a Stoic demeanor throughout his struggle against apartheid and his lengthy prison sentence. Mandela led negotiations with an oppressive and hostile regime by foregrounding justice, maintaining equanimity, and displaying impressive resilience, making him a paragon of Stoic negotiation.

11.5. Stoicism in a Volatile World: An Outlook

As we venture into an increasingly volatile and interconnected world, where disputes range from boardrooms to international borders, we need an anchor more than ever. Stoicism holds the potential to be this anchoring philosophy for us, a constant amidst the changing tides. It helps us to not just sail against the storm, but to do so with unflinching resolve, steady pragmatism, and a masterful sense of control. In the heart of the storm, this philosophy teaches us to be the oasis of calm, inspiring both respect and cooperation towards effective resolution.

In this journey of bridging the past with the future, Stoic negotiation doesn't just stop at being a tool but transforms into a leadership philosophy — moving beyond the confines of a negotiation table, influencing communities, organizations, and nations towards harmonious and constructive engagements, demonstrating the breathtaking potential of this ancient philosophy to shape the future of negotiation.

In a world desperately seeking sound anchors, Stoicism rings true – ancient wisdom for a modern world. It's a philosophy that doesn't run from conflict but embraces it, wrestles with it, and ultimately transforms it into harmony. Stoicism is indeed the lighthouse for the negotiators of the future, a beacon illuminating the path to effectiveness, fairness, and serenity.

www.ingramcontent.com/pod-product-compliance
Lightning Source LLC
Chambersburg PA
CBHW071049260726
48661CB00007B/3231